BOOKER T.
WASHINGTON
INNOVATIVE EDUCATOR

SPECIAL LIVES IN HISTORY THAT BECOME

Signature LIVES

BOOKER T.
WASHINGTON
INNOVATIVE EDUCATOR

by Kristin Thoennes Keller

Content Adviser: H. Tyrone Brandyburg,
Chief of Resource Education and Interpretation,
Tuskegee Institute National Historic Site,
Tuskegee Airmen National Historic Site,
Selma to Montgomery National Historic Trail

Reading Adviser: Rosemary G. Palmer, Ph.D.,
Department of Literacy, College of Education,
Boise State University

COMPASS POINT BOOKS MINNEAPOLIS, MINNESOTA

Compass Point Books
3109 West 50th Street, #115
Minneapolis, MN 55410

Visit Compass Point Books on the Internet at *www.compasspointbooks.com*
or e-mail your request to *custserv@compasspointbooks.com*

Editor: Shelly Lyons
Page Production: Blue Tricycle
Photo Researcher: Svetlana Zhurkin
Cartographer: XNR Productions, Inc.
Library Consultant: Kathleen Baxter

Art Director: Jaime Martens
Creative Director: Keith Griffin
Editorial Director: Carol Jones
Managing Editor: Catherine Neitge

Library of Congress Cataloging-in-Publication Data
Thoennes Keller, Kristin.
  Booker T. Washington : innovative educator / by Kristin Thoennes Keller.
    p. cm. — (Signature lives)
  Includes bibliographical references and index.
  ISBN-13: 978-0-7565-1881-3 (hardcover)
  ISBN-10: 0-7565-1881-4 (hardcover)
  ISBN-13: 978-0-7565-1985-8 (paperback)
  ISBN-10: 0-7565-1985-3 (paperback)
  1. Washington, Booker T., 1856-1915—Juvenile literature. 2. African
Americans—Biography—Juvenile literature. 3. Educators—United
States—Biography—Juvenile literature. I. Title. II. Series.
  E185.97.W4T47 2007
  370.92—dc22   2006002995

Signature Lives

MODERN AMERICA

Starting in the late 19th century, advancements in all areas of human activity transformed the world into a new and modern place. Inventions prompted rapid shifts in lifestyle, and scientific discoveries began to alter the way humanity viewed itself. Beginning with World War I, warfare took place on a global scale, and ideas such as nationalism and communism showed that countries were taking a larger view of their place in the world. The combination of all these changes continues to produce what we know as the modern world.

Table of Contents

Chapter 1

SPEAKING IN ATLANTA

⁓⁓⁓

It was 1895, and people from all over the world had gathered in Atlanta, Georgia, to attend the Atlanta Exposition, a public fair. Ever since the American Civil War ended in 1865, businesses in the South were struggling to survive. Cities, railroads, and farms had been destroyed in the fierce battles. Southern products and services were once again ready to be sold, and the exposition was supposed to help the South by attracting buyers.

Most people in the crowd were surprised to see a well-known black man on the exposition's stage alongside white men. They were even more surprised when he was introduced as the next speaker: "We shall now be favored with an address by a great Southern educator." The audience cheered loudly. When the African-American man rose to speak, the

Booker T. Washington was passionate about educating African-Americans and founded a school in Tuskegee, Alabama.

The grounds of the Atlanta Exposition

applause ceased, and the auditorium fell quiet.

The speaker's name was Booker T. Washington, a strong advocate for the education of African-Americans and the founder of Tuskegee Normal and Industrial Institute, a school for African-Americans. He had been asked to speak as a representative of his race.

Before beginning his speech, Washington looked out at the thousands of eyes staring at him. He knew his speech had to appeal to everyone—blacks and whites. Well aware that racial tension was a problem in the South, he had spent a great deal of time preparing. While the war brought an end to slavery, problems for African-Americans had continued. Some white Americans were violent toward blacks, burning their homes and businesses. In addition, Southern states passed segregation laws that were unfair to blacks.

Booker T. Washington's goal for his Atlanta Exposition speech was "to say something that would cement the friendship of the races and bring about hearty cooperation between them." He had vowed "to say nothing that [he] did not feel from the bottom of [his] heart to be true and right."

Washington began by saying that blacks were one-third of the South's people and that no one should ignore this fact. He urged both races to be friendly to each other and asked white people to hire blacks. He urged that neither race try to upset the other. Washington wanted African-Americans to stop agitating whites in order to acquire equal rights. Instead, he thought, blacks should learn skills that would help them get jobs.

Washington believed blacks should take pride in farming and other service jobs: "It is at the bottom of life we must begin, and not at the top. Nor should we permit our grievances to overshadow our opportunities." Washington believed that hard work, patience, and pride in one's work would pave the way to equal rights. According to him, civil rights should be earned, not given.

As Washington spoke that day, his ideas were met with round after round of applause. When he finished, he enjoyed a standing ovation. The speech helped Washington earn respect from whites. He later recalled that so many people shook his hand it was hard to leave the building. The next morning, he was surrounded by people when he went outdoors. On the way home to Tuskegee, Alabama, crowds of people at each train station wanted to greet him. Washington had grown used to crowds though, especially in Alabama, the state where Tuskegee Institute was located.

What's more, newspapers throughout the country published his speech in full. Washington started receiving invitations to the homes of wealthy white Northerners. Many of them donated money to Tuskegee Institute.

Although Washington gained popularity with whites because of his ideas, many African-Americans were disappointed with his speech. They thought he should have demanded equal rights for blacks. Some thought he was limiting black education to skills training. His critics wanted blacks to be able to choose their own course of study.

Indeed, Washington's ideas were unusual for an African-American living during that time. However, Washington himself had received an education at a trade school. He deeply believed in his ideas for

ADDRESS BY BOOKER T. WASHINGTON, PRINCIPAL

TUSKEGEE NORMAL AND INDUSTRIAL INSTITUTE, TUSKEGEE, ALABAMA,

AT OPENING OF ATLANTA EXPOSITION,

Sept. 18th, 1895.

- - - - - -

Mr. President, Gentlemen of the Board of Directors and Citizens:

One third of the population of the South is of the Negro race. No enterprise seeking the material, civil or moral welfare of this section can disregard this element of our population and reach the highest success. I but convey to you, Mr. President and Directors, the sentiment of the masses of my race, when I say that in no way have the value and manhodd of the American Negro been more fittingly and generously recognized, than by the managers of this magnificent Exposition at every stage of its progress. It is a recognition which will do more to cement the friendship of the two races than any occurrence since the dawn of our freedom.

Not only, this, but the opportunity here afforded will awaken among us a new era of industrial progress. Ignorant and inexperienced, it is not strange that in the first years of our new life we began at the top instead of the bottom, that a seat in Congress or the State Legislature was more sought t an real-estate or industrial skill, that the political convention, or stump speaking had more attractions that starting a dairy farm or truck garden.

An autographed transcript draft of Washington's Atlanta Exposition address

slowly advancing blacks in society. And, though controversial, Washington's speech, its impact, and his life work helped improve the lives of countless African-Americans. ❧

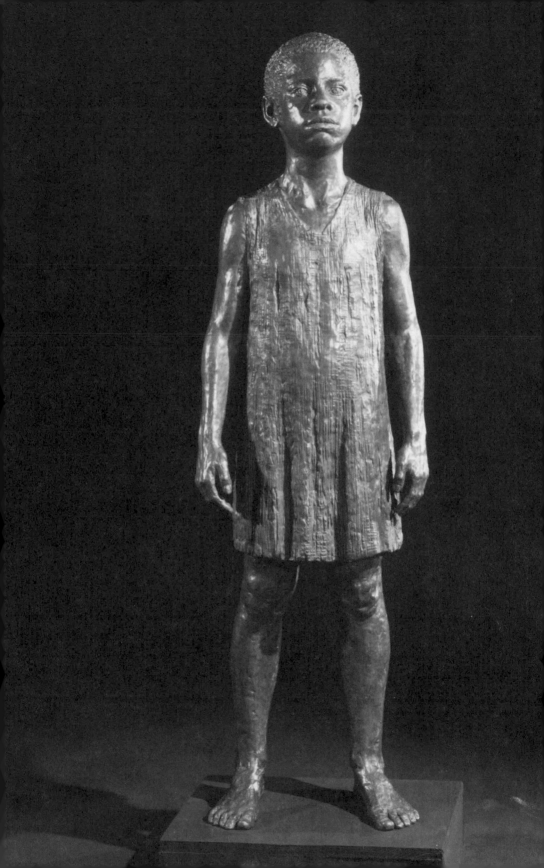

2 LIFE AS A SLAVE

❧❀❧

When Booker T. Washington was born in the spring of 1856, no one expected him to become a leader. Booker was born into slavery. When his mother gave birth to him in a log cabin near Hale's Ford, Virginia, he became James Burroughs' property.

Because he was an enslaved person, Booker was never certain about the date of his birth. He later said, "In the days of slavery not very much attention was given to family history and family records—that is, black family records." Booker knew nothing about his family history beyond his mother. He did not even know his father's name, a white man he never knew.

Booker lived with his mother, Jane, older brother, John, and younger sister, Amanda, in the cabin where he was born. There were no screens or glass panes

Lloyd Lillie's bronze statue of Booker T. Washington was commissioned by the National Park Service in Hardy, Virginia.

The cabin on Burroughs' plantation where Washington was born

in the windows, and the floor of the cabin was bare earth. Booker's bed was a pile of rags on the floor.

The tiny cabin was also used as the kitchen for the plantation. Booker's mother was the plantation cook. She cooked over an open fire for the Burroughs family and the slaves. The cabin was freezing cold in the winter because of the uncovered windows and hot in the summer because of the open fireplace.

As an enslaved woman, Booker's mother worked from morning until night. She had little time to attend to her own children. Booker's earliest memory was of her cooking a chicken late at night and then waking the children to feed them. He never knew how or where she got the chicken, but later in life he assumed she stole it from the Burroughs family. Booker never considered his mother a thief, however, because he understood that she was a victim of slavery.

Washington later recalled that he rarely had any playtime as a child: "From the time that I can remember anything, almost every day of my life has been occupied in some kind of labour." His masters expected him, as a child, to carry water to men in the fields, clean the yards, and fan flies from the master's family while they ate. Later in life, Booker would attend many dinners and formal gatherings. Perhaps he learned table manners and the value of mealtime conversation from his experiences at dinner tables.

Once each week, Booker had to take the corn crop to the mill, which was about 3 miles (4.8 kilometers) from the plantation. He dreaded this work. Along the way, the bag often shifted and fell off the horse. Booker wasn't strong enough to lift the bag of corn onto the horse's back, so he would have to wait for hours until someone passed by to help him. He was afraid of outlaws and often cried while he waited. Sometimes he waited so long that it was already dark when he returned home through the woods.

Slavery made Booker's early years physically and emotionally difficult. He could have grown up to be a bitter man, but Booker chose to live a productive, positive life. ❧

Chapter

3 FIRST YEARS OF FREEDOM

❧❧❧

Booker's last years of slavery were during the American Civil War, which lasted from 1861 to 1865. The issue of slavery, which had been debated since the very beginning of the country, had finally torn the nation in two. The Southern economy was tied to slavery. Plantation owners relied on slave labor to raise crops such as cotton, sugar, and tobacco. The Northern states had banned slavery years earlier but the practice was still widespread in the South.

As the slavery debate raged on, 11 Southern states left the Union to form the Confederate States of America. The resulting Civil War became the most deadly ever fought by Americans. Although the Confederates won some early victories, they could not hold off the stronger Northern force forever.

Issued by Abraham Lincoln, the Emancipation Proclamation took effect in January 1863. It freed enslaved people of the South.

The relationship between the master's family and the enslaved people on the Burroughs' farm was not typical. According to Booker, the enslaved people felt a desire to protect the Burroughs women and children in the absence of the men during the war. The enslaved people gave Northern soldiers food, drink, and clothing. But they never revealed where the Burroughs' silver had been hidden. Later in his life, Booker would encourage friendly relations and cooperation between blacks and whites. His relationship with the Burroughs family may have been the basis for that desire.

Booker recalled later that the enslaved people around him knew freedom was coming. They saw Confederate soldiers who had deserted and returned home, and they heard rumors as news of the war made its way around communities. Even though they longed for their freedom, many did not wish harm upon their masters. In fact, when he heard that Billy Burroughs had been killed in the war, Booker felt that "the sorrow in the slave quarter was only second to that in the 'big house.'" When two other Burroughs boys returned home wounded, some slaves felt it an honor to care for their masters.

Booker remembered the day a stranger came to the Burroughs' farm, telling the slaves they were free. The stranger said they could go where they wanted and when they wanted. Booker—who had been a slave for his nine years of life—recalled "great rejoicing, and thanksgiving, and wild scenes of ecstasy." His mother "leaned over and kissed her children, while tears of joy ran down her cheeks."

For 12 years after the war's end, Union troops occupied the war-torn South. This period was known as Reconstruction and was a time of restoring the unity of the country as well as rebuilding the South. During that time, 17 African-Americans from the South were elected to Congress. Many others served in Southern legislatures. They helped write state laws guaranteeing free public education for all. But when Union troops finally pulled out, they left the former pro-slavery Southerners in charge. Many of the freed

Booker, the young boy with the stick, listened as a stranger read the Emancipation Proclamation to the enslaved people on the Burroughs' plantation.

21

slaves ended up working for their former owners or other whites. Their situations weren't much better than when they'd been enslaved.

Booker's family did not continue to work for the Burroughses. Instead, they set out for Malden, West Virginia, where Booker's stepfather, Washington Ferguson, lived. His mother had married Ferguson after John and Booker were born. "Wash" Ferguson did not live on the same

Near the end of the Civil War, Union troops liberated enslaved people in the South.

farm, so Booker only remembered seeing him at Christmas each year. Ferguson had escaped to West Virginia in 1864. He found work packing salt into barrels in the Malden salt mines near Charleston. When the war ended, Ferguson sent for Jane and the children.

Booker was born near Hale's Ford, moved to Malden, and attended school at Hampton.

The journey to Malden covered hundreds of miles and took several weeks by foot. The family had no money. They placed "what little clothing and few household goods" they had in a cart and set out. Jane's health was poor, so she rode most of the way in the cart while the children walked. Most nights they slept in the open air and cooked over a log fire. One night, they found an abandoned cabin to sleep in. When Jane lit a fire in the fireplace, a long, black snake fell from the chimney and slithered across the floor. The family decided to sleep outdoors that night after all.

> *When slavery ended, the former slaves were elated. Many of them changed their names, which had been given to them by their masters. Many also left their masters' farms and plantations to begin life elsewhere. However, the lives of freed slaves remained difficult because they had no resources to provide food or shelter for themselves.*

Booker was disappointed when they arrived in Malden. The cabin Ferguson lived in was no better than the one they'd left behind. Small, dirty, and uncomfortable, it was among a cluster of tiny, filthy cabins. The smell of garbage and human waste lingered everywhere. Blacks and whites lived side by side, and things could get rough in that environment. Washington later wrote that "drinking, gambling, quarrels, fights, and shockingly immoral practices were frequent."

Within a few days, the boys' new stepfather put them to work in the salt furnaces as salt packers. Booker was only 9 years old. The work was backbreaking. The boys shoveled dried salt into barrels and then pounded down the loose salt until each barrel weighed the set amount. Though they worked hard, the boys did not receive any of the money they earned.

Workers at a West Virginia salt furnace in 1870

Ferguson kept his stepsons' earnings from the mines. It wouldn't be long, however, before Booker would be exposed to what would become a lifelong passion: education. ❧

4 GOING TO SCHOOL

Chapter

—◦◦◦—

Although Booker grew up to be a great educator, he did not have any schooling while he was enslaved. Before the Civil War ended, only white people could receive a formal education. In fact, providing formal education to enslaved people was against the law. Booker did catch a glimpse of school before slavery ended, and it whet his appetite for more:

> *I had no schooling whatever while I was a slave, though I remember on several occasions I went as far as the schoolhouse door with one of my young mistresses to carry her books. The picture of several dozen boys and girls in a schoolroom engaged in study made a deep impression upon me, and I had the feeling*

Booker T. Washington was one of many African-Americans who sought out formal education after the Civil War ended.

that to get into a schoolhouse and study in this way would be about the same as getting into paradise.

Booker's first experience with writing occurred in 1865, when he was working in the salt mines. His stepfather's assigned number as a salt packer was 18. Booker learned to recognize it. Then he traced it in dust or dirt. He did not know any other numbers or letters, but he recalled that learning that number was the beginning of his desire to read and write.

Booker wasn't the only newly freed African-American who wanted to learn to read and write. Many blacks realized the value of formal education. One day, Booker noticed a large crowd gathered around a black man from Ohio who was reading the newspaper aloud. More than anything, Booker wanted to learn to read like that man. Every day on his way home from the salt mines, he would see the man, and Booker would stop to listen to him read.

Because of Booker's interest in reading, his mother somehow found an old spelling book for him. He never found out how she acquired the book. He used it to teach himself the alphabet, but without a teacher, he did not understand letter combinations.

About a month after Booker and his family moved to Malden, an 18-year-old African-American named William Davis moved to town. When the poor black people of Malden realized Davis could read, they

As a young boy, Booker was fascinated as he listened to a man on a street corner read a newspaper.

asked him to teach their children. The families paid him what they could. To save money, Davis taught lessons in a black minister's home in Tinkersville, a section of Malden.

When that school opened, Booker's stepfather did not allow him to attend. Wash Ferguson did not want to pay for Booker's education. Instead, he wanted Booker to keep working at the salt furnaces. The young boy was deeply disappointed. Every day, he looked out from the salt-packing shed to see other children going to and from school.

Soon, Booker joined the night school that Davis organized for adults. Later in life, Booker would be a strong supporter of night school. Booker's mother finally convinced her husband to allow Booker to attend day school if he could work at the salt furnace from 4 A.M. to 9 A.M. It was hard for a young boy to maintain that schedule, but Booker's determination was strong.

In the mid-1800s, more than 50 salt furnaces operated in the Malden area, but Civil War destruction and a flood in 1861 wiped out all but one of them.

Sometime during his first few years in Malden, Booker went to work as a house worker in the home of General Lewis and Viola Ruffner. Booker

left behind the poor conditions of his family cabin and developed a closeness with one of the leading families in Malden. He worked for $5 a month, but all of his wages went to his family.

Booker's relationship with Viola Ruffner was a significant one. Her high standards for good service influenced him and became a foundation for Booker's later philosophies.

I soon began to learn that, first of all, she wanted everything kept clean about her, that she wanted things done promptly and systematically, and that at the bottom of everything she wanted absolute honesty and frankness. Nothing must be sloven or slipshod: every door, every fence, must be kept in repair.

For the rest of his life, Booker couldn't see trash or clutter without wanting to pick it up.

Mrs. Ruffner not only taught him values of cleanliness and order, she also helped him learn to read. She had been a schoolteacher and valued learning. Later, she recalled

On the first evening Booker attended the Tinkersville school, he was asked to recite his name. He noticed that all the children had stated two names at roll call. He didn't know what to say. As a child, he'd only been known as Booker. He blurted out that his name was Booker Washington, perhaps thinking of his stepfather. When Booker was a teenager, his mother told him that his middle name was Taliaferro. Later in life he began referring to himself as Booker T. Washington.

Schools for African-Americans opened up after the Civil War.

that Booker was always willing to study. Impressed with his service and study habits, she allowed him to attend Davis' school a few hours during the day if he got his work done. Mrs. Ruffner also encouraged Booker to start saving books for his own library.

Perhaps one of the most important lessons he learned from her was that anyone could change his or her own social standing. Mrs. Ruffner was from Vermont and had gone to school until she was 17, when she became a teacher. Following that, she became a governess to Mr. Ruffner's children when his first wife died. Later, Mr. Ruffner asked Viola to marry him, and she accepted. Booker saw her story as an inspirational one. He liked that she improved her social status with education and work.

A few times, Booker tried other work, but he always returned to the Ruffners. One of those jobs was in a coal mine near Malden. Booker did not enjoy the work because it was so dark and dirty. He gave up schooling temporarily to work in the coal mine, but he brought his books down the shaft and read by the miners' light whenever he had a spare moment.

Once, while working in the mines, Booker overheard two adult miners talking about another school for black people. The men were talking about the Hampton Normal and Agricultural Institute in Virginia. Booker had not known about any other schools outside of his own in Tinkersville. He learned that those unable to pay could work in exchange for a place to live on campus. Booker set his sights on attending this school. He knew it would offer him a better education than his own school in Tinkersville. ✣

5 HAMPTON INSTITUTE

Chapter

❧⌘❧

Booker T. Washington was 16 years old when he set off for the Hampton Normal and Agricultural Institute in Hampton, Virginia. Because getting an education was very important to Booker, he had the support of the Malden community. As he packed for the 500-mile (800-km) trip, friends came to offer him whatever money they could. With that help, he was able to get halfway to Hampton on the Chesapeake and Ohio Railroad. When he could no longer pay for the train, Booker took the stagecoach, walked, and accepted rides.

By the time he reached Richmond, Virginia, Booker had been traveling several days. He was exhausted and out of money. The hungry teenager slept under a raised sidewalk with his bag as his pillow. In the

Booker T. Washington walked half of the 500-mile (800-km) distance to get to Hampton Institute in Hampton, Virginia.

morning, he gratefully realized he was near shipping docks. There he earned his breakfast by helping on a ship. Booker continued working at the docks until he'd saved up enough money to finish his journey to Hampton, which is on the Chesapeake Bay in southern Virginia. Nothing could get in the way of his quest for an education.

Hampton Institute would offer Booker what he was looking for. The school consisted of a brick three-story building and several barracks. The boys' rooms were on the third floor of the main building. The girls' living quarters were located in one of the barracks. The other barracks served as the dining room, kitchen, and laundry. The classrooms were in the main building.

When Booker arrived at Hampton Institute in 1872, he hadn't bathed or changed his clothing in more than a month. He also arrived after the school year had started. The principal, Mary F. Mackie, hesitated to admit him to the school. She did, however, offer him a room and told him she would decide later whether or not to admit him. Booker cleaned himself and his clothing and returned to Miss Mackie. She asked him

Hampton Normal and Agricultural Institute in the late 19th century

to sweep an adjoining room.

Booker understood that this was to be his entrance exam, and he took it very seriously. Booker swept the room three or four times. Then he dusted it many times before calling Miss Mackie to inspect.

Miss Mackie rubbed her handkerchief over the walls, benches, and tables. She even rubbed it on the woodwork and the floor. Booker had done such a fine job that she found no dirt or dust on the floor or the furniture. She admitted him on the spot and offered him the position of the building janitor.

Hampton was a trade school and a school for future black teachers. The instructors taught students specific skills they could use to earn a living.

Students learned farming, carpentry, bricklaying, and sewing. Booker's trade was that of janitor, which he did throughout his three years there. The janitorial work suited Booker because he was used to performing domestic chores. He liked being in the school instead of out in the barns because he could observe the white teachers at the school. It also gave him closer contact with the head of the school, General Samuel Chapman Armstrong. Armstrong's ideas about education would serve as the model on which Booker would later base his own ideas.

Armstrong was a handsome man with a strong presence. Booker and the other students deeply liked and respected him. Although Armstrong was only in

A shoe-making class at Hampton Institute

his early 30s, he had served the Union in the Civil War. In fact, he had served with such distinction that he was asked to serve as lieutenant colonel over the 9th U.S. Colored Troops. Armstrong fought alongside the other white officers and the black enlisted troops.

After the war, Armstrong wanted blacks to be granted citizenship through education and industry. He offered his assistance to several government agencies and was given responsibilities in 10 counties in Virginia. One of his duties was to take charge of education in those counties.

General Samuel Chapman Armstrong founded Hampton Normal and Agricultural Institute in 1869.

Armstrong believed that African-Americans were "in the early stages of civilization." He thought their moral training was more important than intelligence training. He believed blacks needed to learn self-discipline before they could become more intelligent or spiritual. He thought they needed to learn industrial trades before they could become active in politics. So in 1869, Armstrong established Hampton Normal and Agricultural Institute, where he could teach these ideals.

Armstrong and his teachers stuck to a tight schedule of study, inspections, and prayer. Students marched wherever they went. They were expected to keep themselves clean. During Booker's first week, he learned about bathtubs, toothbrushes, and shoe polish.

The formality and schedule were designed to improve the students' self-discipline. A system of demerits was used as punishment for any student who didn't follow the schedule. While Hampton's main focus was to train its students to become elementary school teachers, Armstrong deeply believed that African-Americans would benefit from discipline and skilled labor. Because of this belief, he allowed students to work at the school to pay for their tuition and board. This also kept costs low at the school.

Booker enjoyed debating in the two or three debate clubs at Hampton. His style was modest. He relied on everyday wisdom in his speaking. He often used stories and jokes to make a point or wrap up an argument. One teacher gave him private lessons in breathing, word emphasis, and articulation. Booker never missed a Saturday night debate meeting. He even organized a group called the *After Supper Club*. The only time they met was during the 20 minutes of free time after supper each evening.

Other than debate, Hampton Institute did not offer much in the way of activities or entertainment.

There were no organized athletics yet. The only social gatherings occurred at the home of the school treasurer, General James Fowle Baldwin Marshall, and his wife, Maria. Once in a while, about 10 boys and girls were selected to spend the evening with several teachers in the Marshalls' parlor. There they played games and had quiet conversation.

General Marshall respected and trusted Booker. After Booker's first year at Hampton, the other students went home for the summer. Booker could not afford the trip. Booker took a job in a restaurant

Hampton students were allowed to work at the school to pay for their tuition and board.

A classroom at Hampton Institute

at a large resort hotel at Fortress Monroe, a military fort near Hampton. But his pay was so low that he could not save anything. At the end of that summer, he told Marshall that he had no money for tuition. Marshall told Booker he could re-enter school and would be trusted to pay the debt when he could.

In the spring of 1874, during Booker's second year at Hampton, his mother and brother sent him money to come home for the summer. Upon returning to Malden, Booker realized the town was experiencing an economic depression. All of the salt furnaces had closed. The coal mines also were closed because of a strike.

After a month of searching for work, Booker walked a long distance one day to find a job, but he had no luck. Starting home after dark, he was so tired that he stopped to sleep in a room of an abandoned salt furnace, about a mile from home. He awoke at about 2 A.M. to find his brother, John, there. John had been searching for Booker to tell him that their mother had died. Booker was devastated.

Booker's family struggled after Jane's death. Booker's stepfather didn't have a job. Twelve-year-old Amanda took over her mother's duties around the house. Booker's old friend Mrs. Ruffner tried to find work around her house for him. By the end of the summer, Booker was again working in a coal mine. He used the money he earned and money his brother gave him to return to Hampton.

Fortress Monroe, or Fort Monroe, is a military fort located in Hampton, Virginia. Fortress Monroe was part of Elizabeth City County until 1963, when it became part of the city of Hampton. The fort, which is named after President James Monroe, is surrounded by a moat and is still used as an Army post today.

In 1875, Booker graduated from Hampton Institute. He was asked to take part in the graduation ceremony. His role was to debate the issue of whether the United States should annex, or take over, Cuba, which was then in rebellion against Spain. Cuba's citizens used black slave labor. Booker's opponent presented arguments that would naturally appeal to most black people of the time. He argued that the United States should annex Cuba, saying it would liberate Cuban blacks. It would do away with the slave trade, and it would increase the number of African-American votes.

Booker surprised everyone with his argument. He was against annexation, saying that the United States already had difficulty dealing with the freedom of 4 million American blacks. He suggested that the United States would be flooded with crime and ignorance. He said Spain had a right to Cuba by discovery and colonization.

Booker's arguments were summed up in the *New York Times* and other newspapers. It was clear that Booker had absorbed many of the ideas and values of General Armstrong.

Booker later believed that Hampton had given him a better education than he would have received in even the country's top schools. He attributed this to the school's industrial emphasis. He believed this gave the students skills to improve themselves and

Booker rehearsed for his graduation debate address. It was his first public speech, but it would not be his last.

a sense of usefulness in their communities. Booker thought that teaching blacks skills and self-respect were the way to improve race relations. He was ready to take those ideals with him into the next phase of his life. ✎

6 EARLY PROFESSIONAL YEARS

༄༅

When Booker T. Washington left Hampton the day after graduation in 1875, he felt nervous. The South was still suffering the effects of the economic depression that had begun two years earlier. Washington knew that he might not find a teaching job until the fall when schools opened again. He might not even find work then. He didn't have many skills beyond houseboy, waiter, and janitor. He decided he would have better luck if he went north.

Washington worked at a hotel restaurant in the New York area. But he was not prepared to wait on such elite and wealthy customers. He did such a poor job of serving his first meal that his customers scolded him. He was demoted to busboy and dish carrier. However, Washington was determined, and he soon worked his way up to the position of waiter again.

Soon after graduating from Hampton Institute in 1875, Booker T. Washington's lifelong passion for teaching was ignited.

In 1875, the United States was experiencing an economic depression that began with the Panic of 1873. This panic was ignited by the failure of the investment firm Jay Cooke & Company. Following this firm's collapse, the stock market shut down for 10 days, banks closed, and factories also began closing. Thousands of Americans lost their jobs. It was the worst economic crisis the United States had ever experienced.

At the end of the summer, he headed to Malden to find a teaching job. But even before he got there, the black families of the Tinkersville school had elected him to be the teacher. During Washington's first year of teaching, the pay was merely survival money. That year in Kanawha County, where Malden was located, white male teachers were paid $41.10 per month, and black male teachers were paid $31.50 per month.

In the fall of 1876, 20-year-old Washington was no longer living with his family. He moved into a little two-room house situated between railroad tracks. He often taught from 8 A.M. to 10 P.M. because he had opened a night school. He knew that many blacks wanted to learn but had to work all day. Washington also taught two sections of Sunday school, one at the Baptist Church and one at a salt furnace.

There were around 85 students enrolled in Washington's day school, and nearly as many enrolled in the night school. Washington had a hard time keeping all of his students motivated and

Washington was a Sunday school teacher and lifelong member of African Zion Baptist Church in Malden.

advancing at their own levels. In addition to teaching, Washington helped his brightest students prepare to enter Hampton. All of these students were boys except one: Fanny N. Smith, who would later play a bigger role in his life.

Washington didn't just teach day school, Sunday school, and night school. He also started a small public library for the black community. And, not wanting to give up his passion for public speaking, he started a debate club. Many blacks enjoyed the club because there was no other public entertainment.

Washington often communicated with his former Hampton teachers. Early on, they sent some textbooks he could use in the classroom. When he wrote to thank them, he asked for any extra newspapers they had. He wanted to have a reading room for his students.

Samuel Chapman Armstrong set an example that Washington would follow.

In his second year of teaching at Tinkersville, he reported to his old teachers that his school was larger than it had been the first year. He told them that he enjoyed teaching because the more he taught, the more he himself understood the subjects.

Like General Armstrong had done at Hampton, Washington required his students to keep their clothing and boots neat and clean, their teeth brushed, and their hair combed.

Washington was popular with both his students and the community. Even though he was strict, he also had a sense of humor. His students later reported how thrilled they were to have a teacher who had once been like them and had gone to college. Two of his former students became lawyers and minor public officials. Another became a doctor and a member of the Boston public school board.

Every year, Washington arranged the school's closing exercises. Children wore new clothing, usually sewn by their mothers, and they either spoke or sang. Most of their parents sat proudly in the audience, pleased their children were receiving an education. Because of his teaching and involvement in the closing exercises, the community knew Washington well.

In 1877, the citizens of West Virginia voted on which city should be the state capital: Charleston, Martinsburg, or Clarksburg. Some Charleston residents wanted greater African-American voter turnout, so they asked Washington to speak to black audiences.

Washington spent that summer on a speaking tour. He shared the platform with his old teacher William Davis and other black speakers. Due in large part to Washington's speeches, the final vote in Greenbrier County was 1,902 votes for Charleston, 4 votes for Clarksburg, and 0 votes for Martinsburg. Statewide, the voters also selected Charleston.

The Capitol building in Charleston, West Virginia, was built in 1885.

Earlier in his life, Washington had wanted to be a lawyer. The success of the Charleston campaign renewed his interest in law. He began reading books that would help him prepare for that career. However, he soon realized he would be able to help more African-Americans as a teacher than he could as a lawyer. So he quickly gave up that career path and, in the fall of 1878, entered Wayland Seminary in Washington, D.C. He was just 22.

Washington found he did not like city life. What's more, he often found himself comparing Wayland to

Hampton, but in an unfavorable way. The students, he thought, had more money, were better dressed, and were sometimes brilliant compared to those he had studied with at Hampton. However, he felt that the activities and requirements of Hampton students helped them build character. They were more prepared for life, he thought, because they worked to provide their own bed, board, clothing, books, and tuition.

While at Wayland, Washington received a letter asking him to speak at Hampton's upcoming graduation ceremonies. In the spring of 1879, Washington traveled by rail to Hampton so he could speak in the ceremony. He called his speech *The Force That Wins*. In it, he urged students to understand that they could either labor and succeed or labor and fail. He told them that education was not enough. They also had to have wisdom and common sense. Their hearts had to be in the right place, and they had to trust in God. Washington said the key to success was not in talking about or planning noble deeds, but in doing them.

Washington went back to Tinkersville, where his brother had become the school's teacher. Within a month of delivering the speech at Hampton, Washington accepted an invitation from Armstrong to teach at Hampton. Armstrong offered him $25 a month and the chance to bring along "a very capable

Once, when accompanying a sick boy on a train, Washington experienced two cases of discrimination. The Native American youth was served a meal, but Washington was not. And at the hotel where the Hampton administrators had told Washington to stay, the clerk said the boy could stay there, but Washington could not. Washington also noted discrimination at Hampton itself, where he was paid far less than the white teachers and was not allowed to eat meals with them.

& deserving but poor student" of Washington's choice. It is believed that Washington chose Fanny Norton Smith, who had dropped out of Hampton earlier in order to earn money to pay her debts to the school.

One of Washington's first jobs at Hampton was to be an on-site house father to about 75 American Indians from the Cheyenne and Kiowa tribes. He lived in the building and oversaw student discipline, studies, clothing, habits, and rooms. He took his duties seriously and felt successful.

By the time Washington completed his first year of teaching at Hampton, the school had been open for 11 years. It was considered the model for trade schools around the country. Armstrong was ready to give Washington another opportunity. Armstrong had realized there were many blacks who couldn't attend school because they had to work during the day. In response, he started a night school at Hampton. Students had to work for 10 hours a day at Hampton and could attend school for two hours each night.

A drawing class at Hampton Institute

Armstrong put Washington in charge of the night school. Washington enjoyed the earnestness and motivation of the students, who had to work so hard for their education. He nicknamed them "The Plucky Class." Washington's night school was so popular that attendance tripled in the first few months. It wouldn't be long, however, before Washington would leave Hampton to begin his own school. ❧

Chapter
7 ARRIVING IN TUSKEGEE

ꙮ

In the early 1880s, many whites wanted to keep all blacks poor and disadvantaged. Some whites wanted blacks to have the freedoms whites did. Still other whites wanted to see blacks educated but only to help the economy. Northerners were the first to set up all-black schools. Eventually, some Southern states saw the need to do this as well.

In 1881, the state of Alabama set aside $2,000 to establish a school in Tuskegee, leaving three trustees with the challenge of finding a teacher. The Alabama school would train black teachers. Because of General Armstrong's work at Hampton Institute in Virginia, Alabama officials wrote to him for advice. They asked if he could recommend a white teacher to be the principal at the new school.

Booker T. Washington opened Tuskegee Normal and Industrial Institute, a school for African-Americans, in 1881.

Armstrong could not think of a suitable white man. However, he wrote back that if they would hire a black man, he could offer them a name: Booker T. Washington. Armstrong went on to give him high praise, writing that Washington was "the best man we ever had here." He also wrote, "I am satisfied he would not disappoint you," and "I know of no white man who could do better."

Armstrong read the return telegraph from the Alabama officials to the Hampton staff and student body, assembled for a chapel service. It read: "Booker T. Washington will suit us. Send him at once." Washington's life work was about to begin.

Washington was 25 years old when he arrived in Tuskegee, Alabama, on June 24, 1881. The town of Tuskegee had 2,000 residents—half were black and half white. The town sat at the southern tip of the Appalachian Mountain chain. Washington had never been to the Deep South before, but he found it pleasant. He was excited about his task.

He was surprised, however, when he realized the school had not even been built. Washington also learned that the $2,000 that had been set aside for the school wasn't available until October. Nor

The *Appalachian Mountains run from Quebec, Canada, to Alabama. The highest mountain in the Appalachian chain is Mount Mitchell, which stands in North Carolina. It is 6,684 feet (2,038 meters) high.*

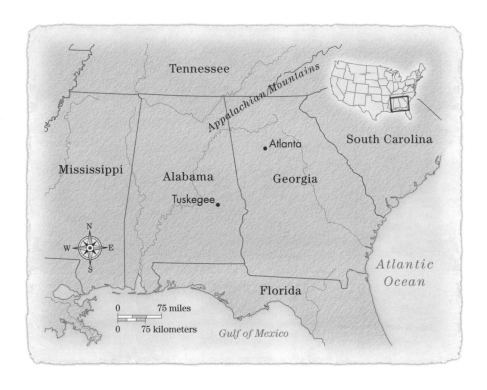

could that money be used for anything but payment of teachers' salaries. No land, buildings, or teaching supplies had been secured. Washington could not purchase books, desks, ink, blackboards, maps, or any of the things he felt he needed for teaching: "The task before me did not seem a very encouraging one," he later wrote.

Tuskegee Institute was built in Tuskegee, Alabama.

Washington had planned to open the school in early July and wanted to stick to his goal. He wrote to his friends at Hampton Institute and asked them to send him whatever books and supplies they could spare. Then he set about looking for a location for the school. He soon discovered a 100-acre (40-hectare) farm south of Tuskegee.

The farmland was hilly and mostly uncleared, but it had an orchard where vegetables could be grown and cotton could be planted. Washington also saw several farm buildings, though in poor shape, which he determined could later be used as small classrooms. The owner, William Bowen, was asking $500 for the property. Washington realized that he had to raise the money for this farm, and fast.

Washington knew that there were some whites who were not supportive of the school, but he was

Three buildings stood on the land that Washington bought. They would house the first classrooms of Tuskegee Institute.

friendly with everyone in town. He did his best to get to know as many people as he could, and he shook hands with a smile whenever he met someone. He also visited two black churches and explained what he wanted to achieve at Tuskegee Institute. Many people came forward after the service to offer their help and encouragement.

One of Washington's tasks at Tuskegee was to choose the students who would enroll. He decided that no one younger than 16 could be admitted. And he selected only those who had already received some education.

Before the Civil War, Macon County, where Tuskegee was located, was one of the richest regions in the state. It had produced a healthy cotton crop, but the war devastated the area. Washington traveled the countryside to see the actual lives of African-Americans. He saw poorly dressed children, overcrowding of homes, poor diets, and overworked families. He knew Macon County needed a school.

Surprising everyone, Washington opened the Tuskegee Normal and Industrial Institute on July 4, 1881, just 10 days after he had arrived in Tuskegee. The school had around 30 students, about half of them men and half women. Classes were held in a shack near the African Methodist Episcopal Church because the farm had not yet been purchased. The shack was in such poor condition that whenever it rained, one of the older students held an umbrella over Washington while he taught.

The Hampton magazine, The Southern Workman, *quoted General Armstrong in 1877 as saying:* "Be thrifty and industrious. Command the respect of your neighbors by a good record and a good character. Own your own houses. Educate your children. Make the best of your difficulties. Live down prejudice. Cultivate peaceful relations with all. As a voter act as you think and not as you are told. Remember that you have seen marvellous changes in sixteen years. In view of that be patient—thank God and take courage."

Washington knew the Bowen farm would be the best place for his school, so he wrote a letter to General Marshall at Hampton, asking to borrow $200. Washington pledged to repay it on October 1 with his own salary, once the funding came through. He told Marshall he wanted to model his school after Hampton. Students would be able to perform labor at the school to pay for their tuition. In doing so, they could help themselves and learn the dignity of labor. Instead of loaning Washington Hampton's money, Marshall sent him a personal check.

Booker T. Washington was a wise man. He quickly bought the farm and had a deed drawn up that stated the school's trustees had the rights to the property. He did not want the land held as state property. That way, he reasoned, if the government took away funding, Tuskegee Normal School could stay open.

Once Washington received the deed to the property, he set to work with his students. He allowed them to pay for the cost of their room and board by

Washington fed the school's chickens with greens from his own garden.

performing chores. Among the chores was making the old buildings usable.

The students and Washington cleaned and repaired the henhouse and horse stable, and turned them into classrooms. They built chairs and desks, and fixed the floors. Residents of Tuskegee dropped off donations the school could use. Maps, textbooks, and newspapers had already arrived from Hampton.

Before starting any classes, however, Washington wanted to clear some woodland for next year's cotton crop. Some of the students were angry about

The buildings and grounds of Tuskegee Institute in the early 20th century

performing more labor. Most had been teachers and considered manual labor beneath them. To show them he was serious, Washington picked up an ax, went out into the woods, and made the first cut.

He and his students spent the next several weeks clearing 20 acres (8 hectares) of land. Unfortunately, they found the land too hilly and sandy to yield a good cotton crop, so they planted vegetables instead.

Once classes began, Washington ran Tuskegee in the same way that Hampton had been run. He insisted that students keep themselves clean, and he required daily inspections. Students had to keep their hair combed and teeth brushed. Men had to wear collars and neckties. The students were busy, but so was Washington. In addition to teaching and monitoring hygiene, he performed all the administrative duties as well.

When he realized it was too much work for one person, Washington asked for help. He sent a letter to Hampton, requesting a few graduates to assist him. One would prove to be especially important. Olivia A. Davidson took the position of Lady Principal at Tuskegee and was in charge of the female students.

Davidson had a gift for raising money. Right away, she organized suppers, benefits, and entertainment for students and enlisted their help in fund-raising. They went door-to-door asking for contributions.

Most of the black residents near Tuskegee were too poor to donate money. But that didn't stop them from giving a chicken, a pie, a pig, or some eggs. Washington said that Davidson never seemed happy unless she was working for black education. With her help, donations began pouring in. By April 1882, one year after Washington had arrived at Tuskegee, the farm and the loans were paid off.

Olivia Davidson was born in Virginia, in 1854. In 1857, she moved with her family to Ohio, where she received an education. She attended Hampton Institute, and in 1879 she received a scholarship to attend Framingham State Normal School near Boston, Massachusetts. Soon after her graduation in 1881, Olivia went to teach at Tuskegee Institute at Booker T. Washington's request.

Olivia Davidson was Lady Principal of Tuskegee Institute.

However, the school still looked more like a farm than a school. It was also lacking basic supplies. There were few dishes and no stove or tables. Students argued about who got to use the only coffee cup. And until the dorms were built, students slept in small cabins with no beds.

For makeshift beds, they sewed large cloth bags together and stuffed them with pine needles. There were no blankets that first year. Some students slept in town with wealthy families. But Washington didn't like that; it was too hard to teach discipline and good hygiene that way.

Washington wanted to construct a building that would contain administrative offices, classrooms, and a dormitory. The estimated cost was $6,000, a great amount of money in those days. To raise the money, Washington and Davidson spent two months touring the Northern states, asking for donations. They were successful.

Washington and Olivia Davidson visited the

homes of known philanthropists, explaining the value of industrial education for blacks. They spoke to social organizations and church groups. By the end of May 1882, they had raised $3,000. This allowed them to begin construction on the new building.

After construction of the new building began, Washington returned to his hometown of Malden. There he married Fanny Smith on August 2, 1882. Fanny returned to Tuskegee with him. Even though she had earned a degree at Hampton, she did not teach at Tuskegee. She gave birth to their daughter, Portia, in 1883. A year later, Fanny died. Historians are not sure what caused her death, though some information exists that suggests she died after falling from a wagon. At the young age of 28, Washington was a widower and single parent. ❧

8 BUILDING TUSKEGEE, BRICK BY BRICK

❦

In the fall of 1882, the first permanent building of Tuskegee Normal and Industrial Institute was inaugurated. It was named Porter Hall, after one of the school's most generous donors. The building had been constructed entirely by Tuskegee's students. Washington felt strongly that they should build their own buildings:

> My plan was to have them, while perform- ing this service, taught the latest and best methods of labour, so that the school would not only get the benefit of their efforts, but the students themselves would be taught to see not only utility in labour, but beauty and dignity.

Tuskegee students used their own handmade bricks to build many of the buildings at Tuskegee Institute.

Porter Hall was the first campus building erected by the students of Tuskegee Institute.

The students were not the only ones who were proud of the building. The local community enjoyed the statewide recognition Tuskegee was receiving. Washington had spent a year trying to convince the white residents that the school was a benefit to the community and not a threat. Finally, people began to see him as someone who could be trusted.

Even though Tuskegee Institute was gaining popularity, the school was always in need of money. Washington spent a great deal of time touring Northern cities, attempting to gain donations. He was very successful at it, but the work was tiring. In 1883, the

Alabama Legislature awarded Tuskegee an additional $1,000 each year to cover staff salaries. Immediately after that, two philanthropic organizations also made generous contributions.

Once the school was up and running, Washington began to change the curriculum. The school's purpose was to train black students to teach in black elementary schools. Courses included history, math, geography, literature, grammar, penmanship, composition, botany, astronomy, and bookkeeping. After two years, Washington added to the traditional curriculum. He wanted to teach the students industrial trades, such as bricklaying and printing. He also wanted to make sure the trades would have value in the Southern economy.

Among the first industrial courses offered at Tuskegee Institute were housekeeping and sewing for the women, and farming, brick making, blacksmithing, carpentry, and printing for the men.

Within a few years, Tuskegee was offering numerous industrial trade courses, such as shoe making, cabinetry, mattress making, broom making, wagon building, painting, and tinsmithing.

Washington always worked the vocations into traditional classes. For example, math students measured the length and width of the floor to determine how much carpet would be needed to cover it. Composition students had to write essays on trades.

A mattress-making class at Tuskegee Institute

Neither Latin nor Greek was taught at Tuskegee. Washington felt that they were useless to everyday life. His approach to black education was simple. He felt that a black person who could offer a useful skill to the community could make a living with that skill. Only then would the white community show that African-American citizen respect.

One of the most successful operations at Tuskegee Institute was the trade of brick making. Brick clay was discovered on the Tuskegee campus. Washington quickly understood that the school could make money while keeping with the values he believed in. He knew there was no brickyard in the town. Because of this, farmers and merchants would buy bricks from the school.

Students built a kiln, and after three failed attempts, finally succeeded in correctly firing the bricks. From that point on, all the buildings at Tuskegee Institute were made from handmade Tuskegee bricks. By 1900, the kiln was making more than a million high-quality bricks each year, which were sold throughout the county.

In 1885, Washington married Olivia Davidson, the Lady Principal of Tuskegee. Together they had two sons: Booker T. Washington Jr. in 1885, and Ernest Davidson Washington in 1889. During their marriage, Olivia kept up her work at the school and her fund-raising efforts in the North. She died of tuberculosis in 1889, three months after giving birth to their second child. Once again, Washington was widowed.

Despite his grief, he continued to work on behalf of Tuskegee. He often invited philanthropists and politicians to visit the school. When they did, they

> *Making bricks is a process that takes time. First, the clay is dug from the ground. Next, large stones are removed from the clay, which is then kneaded like bread dough. After kneading, the clay will be molded into the shape of bricks, and the molds will be laid out to dry. Once dry, the bricks must be fired in a kiln. The heat will remove the water from the bricks and will make them stronger. After the firing process is completed, the bricks are ready to be used for building.*

were always impressed. Tuskegee was enjoying national recognition. Washington's name appeared on a list of the nation's 28 leading college presidents in *Outlook* magazine. Others on the list included the presidents of Harvard, Princeton, and Yale.

In the fall of 1892, Washington married his third wife, Margaret James Murray. She had come to Tuskegee to teach just after Olivia died. Margaret became the Lady Principal and worked with her husband for the good of Tuskegee. She also cared for his three children.

Margaret James Murray became Washington's third wife and a stepmother to his three children.

As Tuskegee continued to grow, Washington longed for an agricultural department. When he moved to Tuskegee, he had toured the farms, introducing himself to the people who lived there. He saw the poverty among farmers who did not know how to rotate crops or grow vegetables. It took him 15 years, but finally he gathered the resources to start the department. In 1896, he hired George Washington Carver to lead it. They later developed the

Margaret and Booker with his sons, Ernest Davidson Washington and Booker T. Washington Jr.

Tuskegee Negro Farmers Conference, which taught farmers how to grow and rotate crops. It also touched on other topics such as the management and care of farm animals. ᗱ

9 Chapter

FAMOUS SPEECH, FAMOUS SPEAKER

⟳∾⟲

While establishing Tuskegee Institute, Booker T. Washington also established himself as a spokesperson for African-Americans. His message to blacks was always the same: peacefully and patiently work your way into white communities. He always assured his white listeners that blacks were willing to contribute to society.

In his speeches, Washington explained that the best way to ease racial tension in the country was to provide formal education for African-Americans. He argued that good teachers and money to pay them would be "more potent in settling the race question than many civil rights bills."

Washington did not have much faith in the federal government ending segregation. He knew that in 1883,

In his speeches, Booker T. Washington urged African-Americans to seek out a formal education as a way to help ease racial tension between blacks and whites.

the Supreme Court overturned the Civil Rights Act of 1875. This act had guaranteed black citizens equal treatment in public places. People such as Frederick Douglass, who was an African-American champion of civil rights, spoke out against the ruling. Washington did not. He insisted on black self-reliance, saying, "Brains, property, and character for the Negro will settle the question of civil rights."

Frederick Douglass was a spokesperson for African-Americans during the 1800s.

Many whites supported Washington's views and contributed money to Tuskegee. Even whites who were members of the Alabama Legislature continued to give more and more funding to the school. Eventually, state officials began asking him for advice. Washington was a positive influence for the improvement of black education.

Even though segregation continued to be a problem, Washington was invited to speak in both the North and the South on behalf of black education. As Tuskegee's enrollment grew and the school became nationally known, more philanthropists made large contributions. Many of these were so generous that they paid for the construction of entire buildings.

Washington's most famous speech was at the Atlanta Cotton Exhibition in 1895, where he was the only African-American speaker on the stage. He encouraged blacks and whites, Northerners and Southerners to "cast down your bucket where you are." He borrowed the phrase from a speech given in 1893 by Hugh M. Browne, a teacher and friend of Washington's. In that speech, at a Thanksgiving service at the Lincoln Memorial Church in Washington, Browne said:

> *I once read of a ship in distress because her fresh water supply was exhausted. Anxiously her crew watched for the approach of some sister ship from which to borrow a new supply. It was not long before the much prayed for ship hove in sight. They signaled to her for fresh water. The answer sent back was, "Cast down your bucket where you are." Thinking they were misunderstood again*

Within 10 years after Tuskegee Normal and Industrial Institute opened, many improvements had been made. The size of the campus had grown from 100 acres to 540 acres (40 to 216 hectares). The number of students had risen from 37 to more than 500. The brickyard was producing thousands of bricks daily. There were new buildings, barnyards, and vegetable gardens. Students were publishing their own small newspaper. And there was a student-built water tower that rose 65 feet (19.8 meters) into the air. It was the highest point in Macon County.

and again they signaled for fresh water,
and again and again came the answer,
"Cast down your bucket where you are."
Finally a sailor cast down their bucket
and to their utter and agreeable surprise
the water was fresh. They were in the
mouth of the Amazon river. For the last
twenty years we have been signaling for
borrowed help; let us now cast down the
bucket where we are. The waters of life are
freely flowing in the condition and environments in which we find ourselves, and
not in the condition and environments of
those to whom we have been signaling.

Washington's speech was titled, "The Atlanta Exposition Address of 1895," but it is often called "The Atlanta Compromise." Some African-Americans believed he asked for less than what he truly wanted for his people. But Washington was expressing his true feelings on how African-Americans in the South could survive in a changing world.

The concept fit nicely with Washington's philosophy of financial independence and personal dignity. He said that black Southerners should not argue for civil rights. Instead, they should keep up their hard work and be patient.

Washington held up his hand during his speech in Atlanta and said that in all things purely social, blacks and whites "can be as separate as the fingers." He spread his fingers far apart before continuing, "yet one as the hand in all things essential to mutual progress." Here he closed his fingers together in a fist. Washington wanted to imply the strength of working together for a stronger economy. He asked Southern whites to give their black neighbors a fair chance.

The fame Washington received from this speech startled him. The text of his speech was reprinted in newspapers across the country. He began receiving requests from newspaper editors to write articles, and he was asked countless times to lecture across the country. He agreed on one condition:

Washington became a new spokesperson for African-Americans.

To all these communications I replied that my life-work was at Tuskegee; and that whenever I spoke it must be in the interests of Tuskegee school and my race, and that I would enter no arrangements that seemed to place a mere commercial value upon my services.

Washington toured the South, speaking on behalf of African-Americans' rights and drumming up funds for Tuskegee Institute.

Washington was soon regarded as the new spokesperson for African-Americans. Frederick Douglass, an outspoken champion of civil rights, had died a few months earlier. Washington's

approach to civil rights, however, was very different from Douglass'. Many African-Americans were disappointed by Washington's passive position. They thought he was only satisfying the white community.

In the years after that Atlanta speech, relations between blacks and whites became tense, particularly in the South. Blacks were not allowed in the same public buildings as whites. Violence against African-Americans frequently occurred. Some laws made it hard for blacks to vote. Even so, Washington continued to repeat the ideas from the Atlanta speech over the next 20 years.

He spoke and worked on behalf of black education and told African-Americans to stop fretting over civil rights. Washington's philosophy was "Don't push." However, as the century came to a close, more black organizations supported pushing for equal rights.

On June 24, 1896, Washington became the first African-American to receive an honorary master's degree from Harvard University. When giving his speech at Harvard, Washington won the crowd over with his humor, and in the end, received a round of applause.

10 SPOKESPERSON FOR HIS PEOPLE

❧∾❧

By 1898, Booker T. Washington was a well-respected educator. He had also become a visible leader and spokesperson for African-Americans. That year, he was invited to speak at the Chicago Peace Jubilee, an event to celebrate the end of the Spanish-American War. President William McKinley was among the 16,000 people in the audience.

In his speech, Washington spoke of black soldiers fighting for their country. He said that a race willing to die for its country should be given the highest opportunity to live for its country. He also made a strong statement about racial prejudice: "I make no empty statement when I say that we shall have, especially in the Southern part of our country, a cancer gnawing at the heart of the Republic, that shall

By the 1900s, Booker T. Washington, a successful speaker and principal, had gained the respect of blacks and whites alike.

one day prove as dangerous as an attack from an army without or within."

After that speech, Washington had lunch twice with McKinley while in Chicago. Newspaper editors challenged Washington because he had dined with the president, a white man. They reminded him that he had often said the races should stay separate socially and should work together only for the economy. The editors wanted to know if Washington was changing his mind about the races mingling socially. He avoided the issue, saying that both races had enough problems without adding a social question. That, he said, would only bring about harm. The incident quickly was forgotten.

By 1899, Washington had been working on behalf of Tuskegee and black education for 18 years. He was exhausted, so he and Margaret took a three-month vacation to Europe. There he had tea with Queen Victoria. He met writer Mark Twain, women's rights leader Susan B. Anthony, and other celebrities and leaders.

Even though Washington enjoyed the break, his thoughts were on the troubles in the United States. The Ku Klux Klan was committing horrible crimes against African-Americans. Some blacks were lynched, and others' homes were burned. The criminals were not being punished. The country, particularly the South, was awash in a tide of fear and rage.

Founded in the mid-1860s, the Ku Klux Klan is a secret society of people who believe the Caucasian race is superior to all other races. The group, which still exists today, often resorts to violence against nonwhites.

A few days before Washington left for Europe, a black man had been accused of murder in Palmetto, Georgia. Angry whites strung him from a tree and burned him alive. African-Americans and their supporters throughout the country were furious.

Washington was asked to make a public statement about what had happened. He did not do so and instead said: "In view of my position and hopes in the interest of the Tuskegee Institute and the education of our people, I feel constrained to keep silent and not engage in any controversy that might react on the work to which I am now lending my efforts." He added, however, that his work offered "the permanent cure for such outrages." Many blacks were deeply disappointed that such a public leader would not comment on the crime. Other black leaders felt resentment toward Washington. They thought he owed it to all blacks to take a stronger stand against racism.

Washington had been a member of the Afro-American Council, a group that fought for African-Americans' civil rights. But he felt the tension rising between him and other, more outspoken leaders. He created his own organization in 1900: The National Negro Business League. The goals of the group were to protect black consumers against fraud, to teach poor blacks about economics, and to promote the achievements of black businessmen. Within a few years, there were branches of the league in major cities across the nation.

Washington also wrote several books during this time. He wanted to further strengthen the public's views about him. One of the books was an autobiography, *Up from Slavery*, published in 1901. The book details the story of his rise from poverty to public life. It was well-received for its inspiring and motivating content.

Up from Slavery was translated into many languages. Its popularity brought about generous donations for Tuskegee Institute. By the end of that

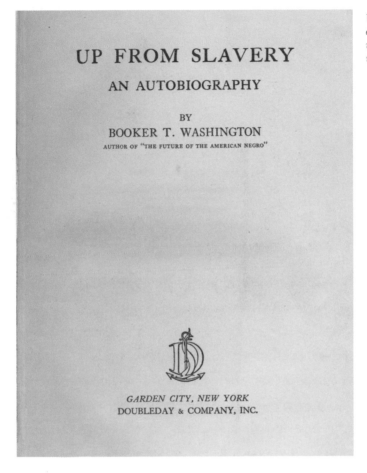

UP FROM SLAVERY

AN AUTOBIOGRAPHY

BY
BOOKER T. WASHINGTON
AUTHOR OF "THE FUTURE OF THE AMERICAN NEGRO"

GARDEN CITY, NEW YORK
DOUBLEDAY & COMPANY, INC.

Washington's autobiography was published in 1901.

year, nearly 1,100 students were enrolled there.

The same year, 1901, President Theodore Roosevelt invited Washington to dine at the White House. Washington's dinner with Roosevelt and his family was met with a public uproar. Critics again attacked Washington for mingling with whites as they did when he had dined with President McKinley. Roosevelt never invited Washington or any other

black guest to dinner at the White House again. But he did rely on Washington's advice in political matters. Washington urged him to appoint blacks to minor federal positions. Sometimes the president acted on Washington's advice; other times he did not.

Washington spent the last 10 years of his life traveling and speaking. His speeches were mostly reworded versions of the Atlanta speech. Wherever he went, he was greeted with enthusiasm. He almost always left a city or town with donations for Tuskegee. The most generous donation came from industrialist Andrew Carnegie, who in 1903 offered Washington $600,000. This was the largest contribution Tuskegee Institute had ever been offered.

Carnegie had said he would donate that amount only if $150,000 were set aside for Washington. Gratefully, Washington held a private meeting with

Carnegie and explained that he could not accept
such a large sum for his own use. Carnegie respected
Washington and gave him the full amount anyway.

That money allowed Washington a much-needed
trip to Europe in September 1903. When he returned
in October, he was refreshed and energetic. He kept a
close eye on Tuskegee Institute, even when he was on
a speaking circuit. Washington would send telegrams
asking for details such as what the students were
eating, how clean the buildings were, and how many
eggs the chickens were laying.

His standards were not only high for the students,
but for the faculty as well. Washington wanted
the academic classes to incorporate the trades
whenever possible. A teacher who didn't comply was
quickly fired. The faculty was frustrated with these
requirements, but they rarely complained because

good jobs were hard to find. Even though there was dissatisfaction within the school, visitors never noticed it. People from all over the world came to observe the campus and were enchanted.

By 1906, various events caused Washington to be deeply disappointed in some of his high-ranking white friends. That year, a shooting in Texas left a white man dead and a police officer wounded. The people blamed black soldiers who were stationed at a nearby army base. Washington urged President Roosevelt to investigate the incident, but Roosevelt simply ordered the dishonorable discharge of all 167 soldiers.

A month later in Atlanta, a mob of white men ran wild for five days, attacking the black community. They destroyed property and killed 10 black men. President Roosevelt did nothing to stop the rioting when it was happening. Again, Washington was disheartened.

In 1909, radical black leaders formed the National Association for the Advancement of Colored People (NAACP). Washington never joined the organization. Other black leaders of the time were angry. They wanted him to support the group because he had achieved such recognition.

Washington stuck to his ideals and stayed focused on Tuskegee Institute. His last contribution to the school was an annual health conference to improve the health and well-being of African-Americans.

By this time, the racial climate in the South was

growing worse. By 1910, lawmakers in Southern states had passed a series of laws that kept blacks from voting. Washington believed that African-Americans who owned property should be allowed to vote. But he also believed that poor, uneducated African-Americans were not qualified to vote. The more political Washington became, the more enemies he made. Angry critics referred to him as the Great Accommodator. Some of his speaking engagements ended in fights and riots.

Washington believed rival black leaders fueled the riots. He kept a list of his enemies and had spies find out what was being said about him. One such enemy was W.E.B. DuBois, who felt that Washington's passive approach to equal rights might have had value in the 1890s, but now was the time for serious agitation. DuBois thought Washington's methods for ending segregation and racism were narrow and ineffective. He also thought that blacks should be encouraged to pursue an advanced education if they wanted.

W.E.B. DuBois was a founding member of the NAACP.

They should not be limited to only an industrial education.

Washington understood his critics. However, he was more concerned with the majority of African-Americans who couldn't read or write. He continued to believe that they needed to master a skill that would help them become respected citizens.

DuBois tried to replace Washington as an African-American leader. It didn't work. Washington had the support of prominent whites, including the steel industrialist Andrew Carnegie and oil baron John D. Rockefeller, who each generously donated to Tuskegee. Washington remained the most visible black leader in the country.

Postage stamps honoring Washington were issued in 1940 and 1956. Also in the 1940s, his face was on the half dollar. He was the first African-American to be pictured on a postage stamp and a coin. And in 1956, the Booker T. Washington National Monument in Hardy, Virginia, was dedicated.

In his later years, Washington became more outspoken about the discrimination and violence blacks continued to face. He complained about inadequate schools and argued for African-American voting rights. Washington's rivals, while grateful, felt that his efforts came too late. They thought his years of taking a passive approach had made people deaf to his message.

In November 1915, Washington was in New York raising money for Tuskegee Institute when he became ill. It isn't clear what his illness was. He entered St. Luke's Hospital on November 4, and stayed there until November 12. He grew weaker each day. Realizing the seriousness of his situation, he wanted to go home: "I was born in the South, I have lived and labored in the South, and I expect to die and be buried in the South." His wife, Margaret, helped him take a train back to Tuskegee. Washington died several hours after reaching his home. His family surrounded him.

Booker T. Washington, who died at age 59, is remembered as an inspiring speaker and educator.

More than 8,000 people attended Booker T. Washington's funeral. The ceremony was simple and humble, reflecting the life he had lived. He had asked to be buried in the Tuskegee campus cemetery and had wanted his gravestone to carry simply his birth and death dates. These requests were honored. The gravestone chosen, however, was very large, perhaps reflecting the big impact Booker T. Washington had on education for African-Americans. ✍

WASHINGTON'S LIFE

1856

Born into slavery on a farm in Franklin County, Virginia

1865

Freed with all other enslaved people when the Civil War ends; moves to Malden, West Virginia, where he first attends school

1872

Enrolls at Hampton Normal and Agricultural Institute in Hampton, Virginia

1865

1865

Lewis Carroll writes *Alice's Adventures in Wonderland*

1856

The Treaty of Paris ends the Crimean War, which was fought between Russia and the armies of Britain, France, Sardinia, and the Ottoman Empire (modern-day Turkey)

1873

Ivy League schools draw up the first rules for American football

WORLD EVENTS

1875

Graduates from
Hampton Institute;
begins teaching in
Tinkersville,
West Virginia

1878

Attends Wayland
Seminary in
Washington, D.C.

1879

Returns to Hampton
Institute to teach

1875

1876

Alexander Graham
Bell makes the first
successful telephone
transmission

1879

Thomas Edison
invents electric lights

WASHINGTON'S LIFE

1881

Opens Tuskegee
Normal and Industrial
Institute in
Tuskegee, Alabama

1882

Marries first wife,
Fanny Smith

1883

Daughter, Portia, is
born

1880

1881

Clara Barton founds
the Red Cross

1883

Brooklyn Bridge
opens to traffic
after 14 years of
construction

WORLD EVENTS

1885

Marries second wife, Olivia Davidson; son Booker T. Jr. is born; his first students graduate from Tuskegee

1889

Son Ernest Davidson is born; Olivia Davidson Washington dies

1884

Fanny Smith Washington dies

1885

1884

The first practical fountain pen is invented by Lewis Edson Waterman, a 45-year-old American insurance broker

1886

Grover Cleveland dedicates the Statue of Liberty in New York Harbor, a gift from the people of France

1889

The Eiffel Tower opens in Paris, France

WASHINGTON'S LIFE

1892

Marries third wife, Margaret Murray

1895

Delivers his famous speech, "The Atlanta Exposition Address of 1895," at the Atlanta Cotton Exhibition

1900

Founds the National Negro Business League

1895

1893

Women gain voting privileges in New Zealand, the first country to take such a step

1896

The first modern Olympic Games are held in Athens, Greece

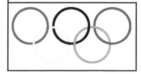

1900

First rigid dirigible is built by Ferdinand von Zeppelin

WORLD EVENTS

1901

Up from Slavery is published; dines with President Theodore Roosevelt at the White House

1906

Celebrates the 25th anniversary of Tuskegee Institute

1915

Dies at home on November 14

1915

1901

Britain's Queen Victoria dies

1906

Earthquake and fires destroy most of San Francisco; more than 3,000 people die

1914

Archduke Francis Ferdinand is assassinated, launching World War I (1914–1918)

DATE OF BIRTH: 1856

BIRTHPLACE: Near Hale's Ford,
Franklin County, Virginia

FATHER: Unknown

MOTHER: Jane (?–1874)

EDUCATION: Malden, West Virginia,
and Hampton Institute

FIRST SPOUSE: Fanny Norton Smith
(1858–1884)

DATE OF MARRIAGE: August 1882

CHILDREN: Portia (1883–1978)

SECOND SPOUSE: Olivia Davidson
(1854–1889)

DATE OF MARRIAGE: August 1885

CHILDREN: Booker T. Washington Jr.
(1885–1945)

Ernest Davidson
Washington (1889–1938)

THIRD SPOUSE: Margaret James Murray
(1865–1925)

DATE OF MARRIAGE: 1892

DATE OF DEATH: November 14, 1915

PLACE OF BURIAL: Tuskegee Institute

FURTHER READING

Haskins, Jim, ed. *Black Stars of Civil War Times: African Americans Who Lived Their Dreams*. Hoboken, N.J.: John Wiley & Sons, 2003.

Schroeder, Alan. *Booker T. Washington: Educator and Racial Spokesman*. Philadelphia: Chelsea House, 2005.

LOOK FOR MORE SIGNATURE LIVES

BOOKS ABOUT THIS ERA:

Amelia Earhart: *Legendary Aviator*
ISBN 0-7565-1880-6

Thomas Alva Edison: *Great American Inventor*
ISBN 0-7565-1884-9

Langston Hughes: *The Voice of Harlem*
ISBN 0-7565-0993-9

Wilma Mankiller: *Chief of the Cherokee Nation*
ISBN 0-7565-1600-5

J. Pierpont Morgan: *Industrialist and Financier*
ISBN 0-7565-1890-3

Eleanor Roosevelt: *First Lady of the World*
ISBN 0-7565-0992-0

Franklin Delano Roosevelt: *The New Deal President*
ISBN 0-7565-1586-6

Elizabeth Cady Stanton: *Social Reformer*
ISBN 0-7565-0990-4

Gloria Steinem: *Champion of Women's Rights*
ISBN 0-7565-1587-4

Amy Tan: *Writer and Storyteller*
ISBN 0-7565-1876-8

On the Web

For more information on *Booker T. Washington*, use FactHound.

1. Go to *www.facthound.com*
2. Type in this book ID: 0756518814
3. Click on the *Fetch It* button.

FactHound will find the best Web sites for you.

Historic Sites

Tuskegee Institute National Historic Site
1212 W. Montgomery Road
Tuskegee Institute, AL 36088
334/727-3200
Museum, historical campus buildings, and Washington's home

Booker T. Washington National Monument
12130 Booker T. Washington Highway
Hardy, VA 24101
540/721-2094
Burroughs' plantation site with historic buildings, trails, and educational programs on slavery

agitating
stirring up public discussion

American Civil War
the war between the Southern states and Northern states, from 1861 to 1865

annex
to add or attach to something larger

articulation
the act of expressing oneself clearly

deed
a signed document containing a legal transfer of property

demerits
marks against someone, usually given for doing something wrong

depression
a period during which businesses, jobs, and stock values decline or stay low

donations
gifts or contributions

dormitory
a building with many separate sleeping rooms

economy
the way a country runs its industry, trade, and finance

exposition
a public exhibition or show

institute
a school that is set up for special purposes

passive
tending not to take an active or dominant part

philanthropists
people who donate money to individuals or causes

prejudice
hatred or unfair treatment of a group of people
who belong to a certain race or religion

racism
the belief that one race is better than another

salt mine
a tunnel where people dig up salt

segregation
the practice of separating people of different races

trustees
people to whom property is legally transferred
to be administered for the benefit of a person or
organization

Chapter 1

Page 9, line 13: Louis R. Harlan. *Booker T. Washington: The Making of a Black Leader, 1856-1901.* New York: Oxford University Press, 1972, p. 216-217.

Page 11, line 21: Booker T. Washington. *Up From Slavery: The Autobiography of Booker T. Washington.* New York: Carol Publishing Group, 1989, p. 220.

Page 11, sidebar, line 4: Ibid., p. 217.

Page 11, sidebar, line 10: Ibid., p. 211.

Chapter 2

Page 15, line 8: Ibid., p.2.

Page 17, line 4: Ibid., p.5.

Chapter 3

Page 20, line 13: Ibid., p. 13.

Page 20, line 26: Ibid., p. 23.

Page 20, line 27: Ibid.

Page 23, line 9: Ibid., p. 25.

Page 24, line 18: Ibid., p. 26.

Chapter 4

Page 27, line 8: Ibid., p. 6–7.

Page 31, line 9: Ibid., p. 43–44.

Chapter 5

Page 39, line 20: *Booker T. Washington: The Making of a Black Leader, 1856-1901*, p. 61.

Chapter 6

Page 53, line 24: Ibid., p. 100.

Chapter 7

Page 58, line 5: Ibid., p. 110.

Page 59, line 6: *Up From Slavery: The Autobiography of Booker T. Washington*, p. 110.

Page 62, sidebar: *Booker T. Washington: The Making of a Black Leader, 1856-1901*, p. 74.

Chapter 8

Page 69, line 8: *Up From Slavery: The Autobiography of Booker T. Washington*, p. 148.

Chapter 9

Page 77, line 12: *Booker T. Washington: The Making of a Black Leader, 1856-1901*, p. 161.

Page 78, line 14: Ibid.

Page 79, line 19: Ibid., p. 212.

Page 80, line 25: Ibid., p. 218.

Page 82, line 1: *Up From Slavery: The Autobiography of Booker T. Washington*, p. 226–227.

Chapter 10

Page 85, line 12: *Booker T. Washington: The Making of a Black Leader, 1856–1901*, p. 237.

Page 87, line 8: Ibid., p. 263.

Page 95, line 11: Louis R. Harlan. *Booker T. Washington: The Wizard of Tuskegee, 1901–1915.* New York: Oxford University Press, 1983. p. 454.

Baker, Houston A. Jr. *Turning South Again: Re-thinking Modernism/ Re-reading Booker T.* Durham, N.C.: Duke University Press, 2001.

Denton, Virginia Lantz. *Booker T. Washington and the Adult Education Movement.* Gainesville: University Press of Florida, 1993.

Harlan, Louis R. *Booker T. Washington: The Making of a Black Leader, 1856–1901.* New York: Oxford University Press, 1972.

Harlan, Louis R. *Booker T. Washington: The Wizard of Tuskegee, 1901–1915.* New York: Oxford University Press, 1983.

Washington, Booker T. *Up from Slavery: The Autobiography of Booker T. Washington.* New York: Carol Publishing Group, 1989.

Kristin Thoennes Keller has written more than 25 nonfiction books for children. She also enjoys writing short stories and essays for adults. Kristin likes cooking, swimming, reading, running, and spending time with her family. Kristin lives in Minneapolis, Minnesota.

Image Credits